CREATIVE WRITING CAROUSEL

WRITTEN BY DORIS SPIVACK
ILLUSTRATED BY ITOKO TAKEUCHI

Cover illustration by Beverly Armstrong

The Learning Works

CONTENTS

Introduction

Creative Writing Carousel is a merry menagerie of imaginative and interesting subjects to motivate students in grades 4 through 6 to write, and to give them topics to write about. Within its covers are

- feet to be followed
- greeting cards to be designed
- menus to be made
- opinions to be surveyed
- questions to be asked
- feelings to be felt
- sensations to become aware of
- experiences to be described
- poems to be composed
- products to be sold
- conversations to be written
- stories to be told

All are designed to encourage students to express their perceptions, thoughts, and feelings while increasing their creative writing skills.

Name ______________________

What's a Noogle?

You have just acquired a new addition to your life. It is a **NOOGLE**. Write about it.

What is a NOOGLE? Is it a pet? Is it a wild animal? Is it a new friend from another country? Is it an invention?

What do you like best about your NOOGLE? Is it kind and loving? Can it sing or tell riddles? Is it skilled at math or at digging holes? Can it wiggle its ears or hang upside down from a branch?

What do you do with your NOOGLE? Can it play games with you? Can it read and write and count backwards from 100? Can you teach it to talk? Can it be programmed?

Design a home for your NOOGLE. Decide how large the structure will be and draw a picture of it, indicating the dimensions. Or, construct and paint a NOOGLE HOUSE. What is your NOOGLE'S favorite color?

Share ideas with a friend. Sometimes two NOOGLES are better than one!

Name ______________________

Decisions, Decisions

Pick one or more of the following topics and write.

What would you do if you had —

- a pen with invisible ink?
- a personal computer?
- no need for sleep?
- a video game arcade?
- a photographic memory?
- a chance to be the leader of your country?

How you would —

- invent a better way to do homework.
- think of ways to stop boredom.
- find a job for the summer.
- write a novel and describe the topic.
- help end world hunger.

Name ____________________

S-T-R-E-T-C-H-I-N-G Your Vocabulary

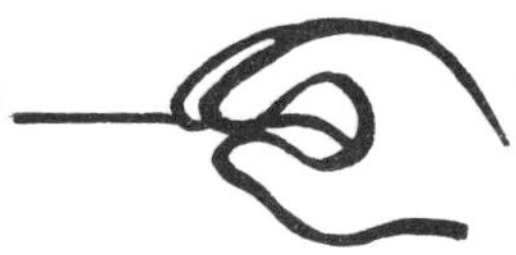

Use a dictionary or thesaurus to find the meanings of the words in bold type, and complete these activities.

- Describe the most **luminous** thing you have ever seen.

- What was so **luscious** that you ate it all, even though you felt **gluttonous**?

- Tell about the **grumpiest** or most **defensive** person you know.

- When did you last feel either **undaunted** or **humiliated** and why?

- Can you combine some of these new words and ideas and meanings to write a **provocative** story? Try it!

Name ____________________

HOBBY HABITS

Choose one of these two ways to describe a favorite interest or hobby.

- Write a detailed paragraph about your hobby.

Example: "My hobbies are collecting baseball cards, coins, and stickers. I have about twenty-five packs of cards. My favorites are a 1956 Mickey Mantle and a 1969 Willie Mays. I have coins from India, Mexico, and America. I'm hoping they will be worth a fortune someday! My best stickers are Googly-eyed Changeables."

- Write a mystery paragraph about your hobby. By the end of your story, the reader should have some clear ideas about what your hobby is. Provide clues.

Example: "I move swiftly out of the big car. I look to the top of the car. I remove my instruments. I walk toward my big, white victim. It is very cold. But I am prepared with special clothing, hand and foot coverings, and glasses. I buy a ticket. I sit and wait. Then I move slowly to the top. I need great physical skill and balance for my hobby. I slide with a graceful energy. What is my hobby?"

Name ______________________

MYSTERY BLOTS

Materials

9″ x 12″ or 12″ x 18″ construction paper
tempera paints or ink
paintbrushes
straws

What You Do

1. Fold your piece of paper in half, then unfold it so that it lays flat.
2. Choose a color of paint or ink and experiment with dribbling or carefully spattering it on one half of the paper.
3. See what different effects you can create. Try blowing the paint or ink around the paper using a straw.
4. Fold the blank half of the paper onto the painted side, being careful not to let the paint run. Press the two sides together gently.
5. Open the paper to discover your mystery blot.

Just for Fun

1. Make several blots and choose one to use as the subject of a story or poem.
2. Turn the paper in different directions, looking for familiar designs in the colored or blank spaces. Do you see a spider . . . a flower . . . a butterfly? Look carefully for clues in your blot.
3. Write a short story or poem about the shapes you see, or write a mystery story using the blot as the major clue.

Name ______________________________

Commercial Time

Study television commercials while watching an hour of television. Time the commercials, and note how frequently they are played. (The average commercial is thirty seconds long, and the product name is usually repeated three to six times.) Notice

- how often the show is interrupted to sell a product
- what commercials you like best and why
- what visual devices are used
- how many people appear in the commercial
- what words or phrases stick in your mind.

Write your own thirty-second commercial for a product not already advertised on television. Repeat the product name three to six times within the message. Rehearse the commercial, timing yourself to make sure you stay within thirty seconds. Perform your commercial for your class.

Name ____________________

SALESMANSHIP

Study newspaper and magazine advertising. Notice which ads catch your eye, how the product is displayed, and any slogans that are used. Make a collection of those that you think are superior. Look for

- good color
- interesting layout
- clever wording
- a product that appeals to you
- information on cost, size, specifications, and deadlines.

Think up your own original product and choose a name for it. Then write an advertisement for the product.

Suggestions:

- a breath mint that colors your mouth red
- windshield wipers on glasses
- an automatic flyswatter
- a mechanical homework-doer
- a robot to make your bed and take out the garbage
- a fuel-less car
- a telephone that you can wear on your wrist
- a chewing gum that contains all the nutrients so meals will no longer be necessary

Decide if the product will be sold in newspapers or magazines. Then design and draw the ad. As you do so, keep in mind the five characteristics listed at the top of this exercise.

Name ____________________

What Can Hands Do?

Trace your hands on a piece of paper. Within their shapes, write about things your hands can do.

Examples: "My hands are good at flying kites. They hold the ball of string just right . . . not too tight or too loose. They feel proud when the kite catches the wind and flies high!"

"My hands can draw pictures of knights and dragons. They are crazy about medieval days! They prefer to use a pen, but my hands aren't bad with paint either."

"My hands like to catch footballs, and they are pretty good at it too! But if they're slippery or cold, sometimes they miss. Then I don't know who feels worse, me or my hands!"

"My favorite hands belong to my Mom. She uses them to bake brownies and pumpkin pies."

"My favorite hands belong to my Little League coach. The signals he makes with them are so funny that sometimes none of us can tell what he means!"

MY HANDS

Name ______________________________

ARE HOLDING . . .

Draw an outline of a special object, invention, or gift. Within the outline, describe the object by writing about its size, color, and texture, and explaining why it is special.

Name ______________________________

Mystery Feet

Trace your feet on a piece of paper. Within their shapes, write about the interesting places your feet have been and what has happened there. Here are some suggestions.

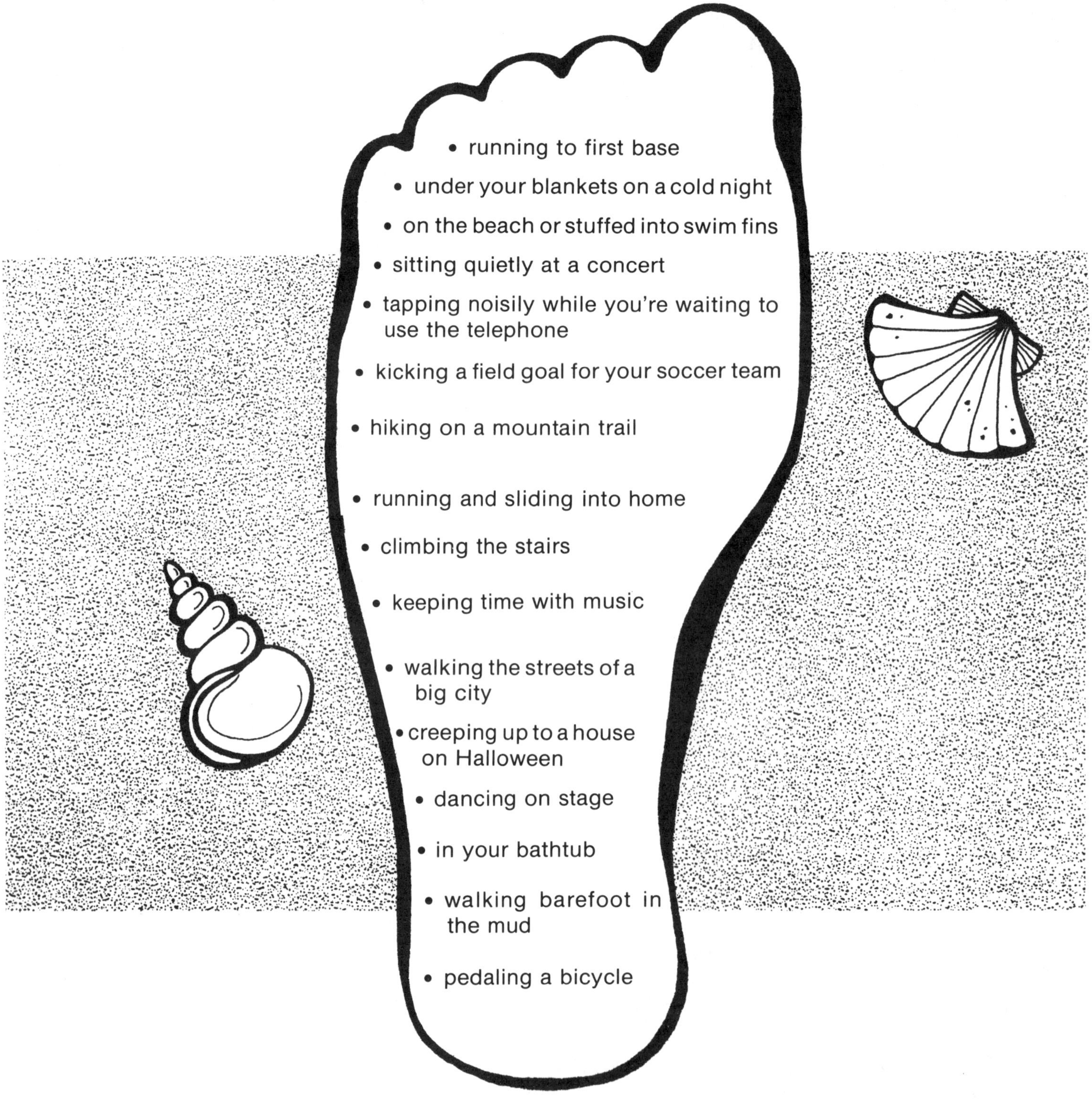

Name ______________________________

BALLOONS

As you look at one of your balloons, you can suddenly see inside it a picture of what you'll be doing five years from now. Write a story about what you see and what your life will be like.

Describe where you would go if you had a magical balloon. Describe the place and tell why you would choose it. Would you take anyone with you? How would you live? How long would you stay?

Twenty friends are coming to your party, and you will give each of them a "Chinese fortune balloon." Write twenty fortunes to place inside the balloons.

Make a colorful montage with magazine pictures of favorite places to visit in a magical balloon. Use tissue paper and starch or draw pictures with crayons and felt-tipped pens.

Imagine you have five balloons to give to five special friends. Write a story about who will receive the balloons and why each friend is so special and important to you.

Name ______________________________

ILLUSTRATING IDIOMS

Write a story or play using as many of the following idioms as possible. Develop visual ideas by illustrating the idioms, and then act out your story for your classmates.

- He's driving me up a wall.
- She's going bananas.
- Hold your horses!
- I'm stuck on you.
- Let's hit the hay.
- He kicked the bucket.
- He's laughing his head off.
- Keep your shirt on.
- Get off my case.
- Does the cat have your tongue?
- She flew the coop.
- Don't beat around the bush.
- Put on your thinking cap.
- Go jump in the lake.
- Go fly a kite.
- It's as easy as pie.
- It's raining cats and dogs.
- Keep your hopes up.
- I'm tied up until noon.
- He's on the ball.
- They are underdogs.
- She cried her eyes out.
- Don't spill the beans.
- He has ants in his pants.
- He knocked his block off.
- He carried on.

Name ______________________

Greetings

Design and write a special greeting card using prose or poetry. If you write rhyming verses, be sure they make sense. Here are some categories from which to choose:

- Get Well
- Happy Birthday
- Thank You
- Friendship
- From the Class
- What Are You Up To?
- Congratulations
- Have a Good Trip
- Valentine's Day
- Christmas, Hanukkah, or New Year
- Just for Fun
- Please Write

Be sure your greeting card fits into a standard size envelope, either 3½″ x 5½″ or 4″ x 10″. Use your best printing, writing, or calligraphy. Design a logo or use your initials on the back of the card.

Name ______________________________

MOODS

To describe various moods and emotions in your stories, it is necessary to know descriptive, expressive words. Most of these words are adjectives, words that describe.

1. Make a list of mood words to describe people, places, and things. You can use this list whenever you write!

2. Write a paragraph in which you describe the mood of a particular place or time.

   Suggestions:

   - in a store at noon
   - in a store at midnight
   - alone in your room
   - taking a walk in the park
   - at the World Series
   - in a space shuttle
   - at a pizza parlor
   - minutes before a final exam

Name ______________________________

ACROSTIC VERSE

Use the letters of your name to write a poem describing yourself. Do the same with the names of your friends or with the names of animals.

Examples:

Doris

Doris likes teaching
Or drawing or swimming or
Reading what others write
If they are doing their best and
Show creativity.

Brian

Brian is bashful and brainy and
Really a good reader, and he's
Into sports a lot. He likes
Apple pie and steak and
Never misses a meal!

Cats

Cats are warm
And friendly. Also,
They are very
Smart.

Elephants

Elephants
Like peanuts,
Especially roasted, salted
Peanuts in the shell.
Hand an elephant peanuts,
And he'll love you.
Never give him peanut butter!
This would make his trunk
Sticky.

Name ______________________

DESIGN A MENU

Study the menus at local restaurants so that you can compare different layouts and designs. Sketch the menus, noting the colors used, the illustrations, the sizes and styles of type, and the placement of the restaurant name. Is the name of the restaurant easy to remember and easy to read?

Study the contents of the menus and the categories of food. You may find

- appetizers
- soups
- salads
- omelets
- sandwiches
- vegetables
- meats
- fish
- poultry
- side orders
- desserts
- beverages

Compare prices at your favorite restaurants. Do not include fast-food restaurants.

Check the size of the menus. Is 5″ x 8″ a comfortable size to hold? Could you design a menu that is larger or smaller, perhaps in the shape of a fish, a hamburger, a pizza, a cow, or a soda?

Design and make your own menu containing your favorite foods. If you decide on ethnic foods (Chinese, Thai, Italian, Mexican, French), you may need to research the names and spellings of the items you'll include.

Add descriptive phrases and illustrations to make your menu mouth-watering.

Name ______________________________

Gifts and Giving

Choose one of the following situations and write a short story about it.

- A member of your family is having a birthday, and you have no money to spend on a gift.
- When you open the presents at your birthday party, you find that three people have given you the same thing.
- You send a very nice present to a good friend, but you never receive a thank-you note or any indication that the gift has been received.
- You inherit one million dollars on the condition that you must give $100,000 of it to deserving community organizations.

Name ______________________

THE CASE OF THE COPPER PENNY

Using the oldest penny you can find, write a mystery story about your coin. Make some decisions before you start to write.

- Who owned the penny and whose lives has it touched?
- When and where did they live?
- Was this penny involved in a burglary? a swindle?
- Was it ever traded, lost, or buried?
- Was it part of a collection to buy something special?
- What is the future of your mystery coin?

Tape your penny to your story.

Name ______________________________

Assemble a Monster

Trace these shapes on tagboard. Enlarge them. Change them. Create some additional shapes of your own. Decorate them with felt-tipped pens. Fasten them together with brads (to make a movable monster!) or glue them to another piece of paper.

Now, write about the monster you have created. Name it. Tell where it lives. Describe its habits, adventures, likes and dislikes, friends and enemies. Involve it in a story.

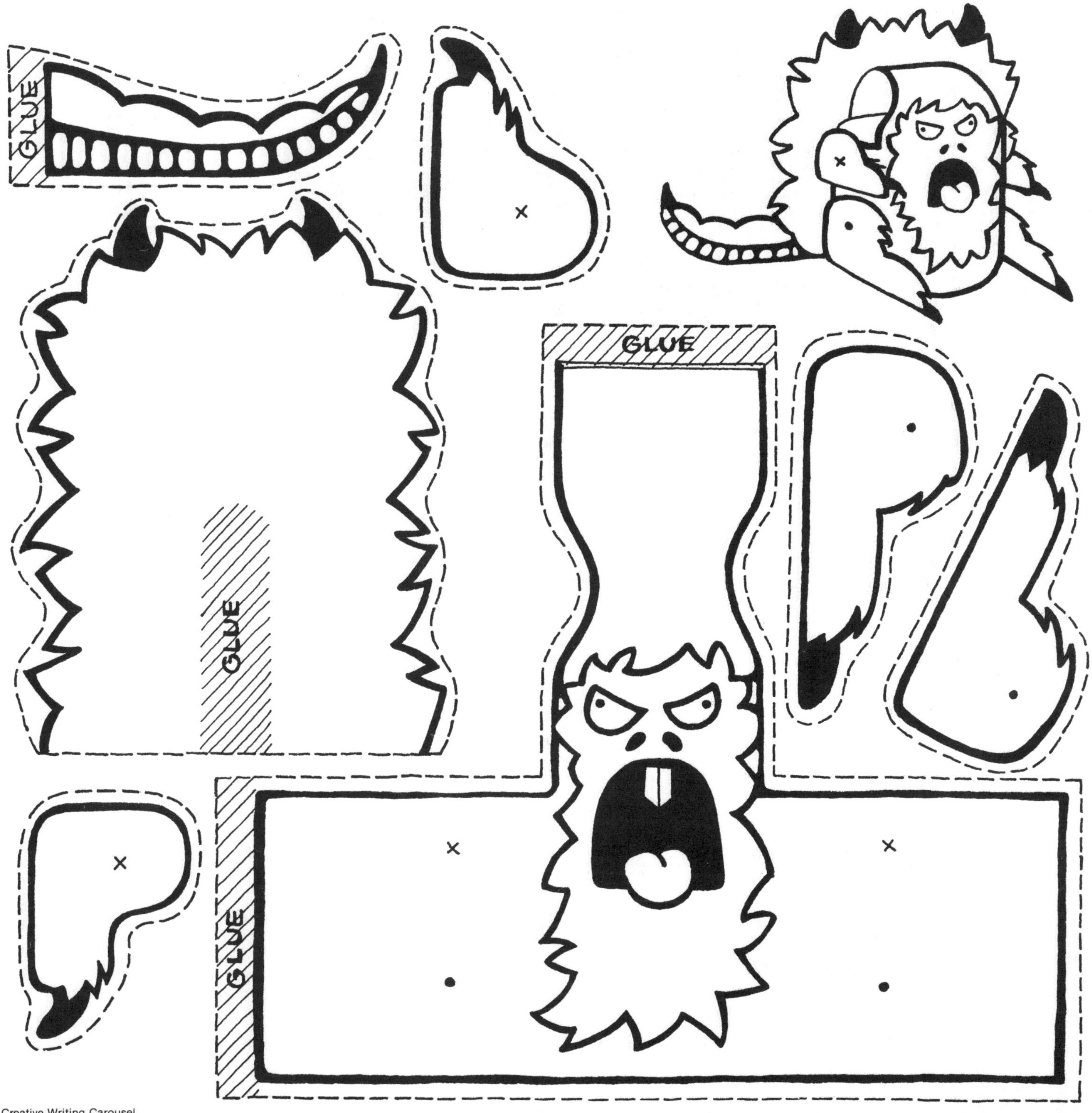

Name ___________________________

Express ideas about yourself in a poem by using words and phrases cut from magazines and newspapers. Collect the words that describe your personality, your thoughts, your feelings, and your ambitions.

Arrange your words carefully on a sheet of paper and glue them on securely. If necessary, add extra words with felt-tipped pens.

Show your poster poem to your classmates, and explain how it represents you.

Name ______________________________

Coat of Arms

Create a coat of arms for yourself by tracing the outline below onto another sheet of paper, then filling in the spaces with the appropriate pictures or symbols.

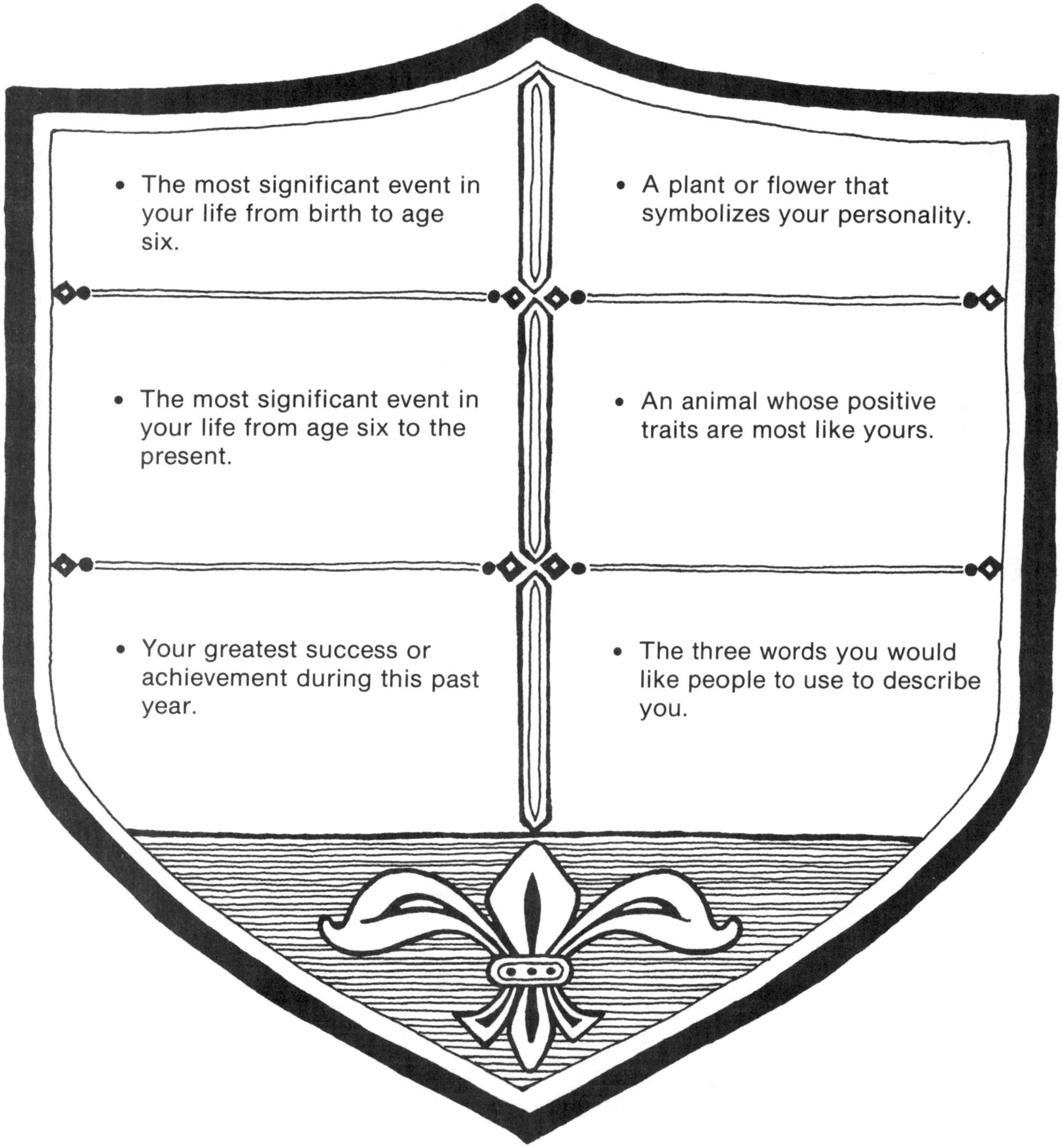

Now, imagine that you become a respected and beloved leader of the people in your country. Write a story about how this coat of arms gains worldwide recognition.

Name ______________________

Lunch Crunch

Lunchtime is a good opportunity to get in touch with your five senses: seeing, touching, smelling, tasting, and hearing. Arrange to have the following kinds of foods for lunch one day:

- peanut butter and jelly sandwich, egg salad sandwich, tuna salad sandwich, or chicken salad sandwich
- celery, carrots, or tomato
- orange or banana
- milk or other beverage

As you eat your lunch, pay attention to the following sensations. Take notes as you bite, munch, sip, chew, swallow.

1. **Look** at the food items. Note the colors, sizes, and shapes.
2. **Feel** them. Note how they feel in your hands, then in your mouth as you eat them. Are they hard, soft, crunchy, or mushy?
3. **Smell** them. Could you identify them with your eyes closed? Describe the smells. Are they pleasant or unpleasant?
4. **Taste** them. Are they sweet, sour, bitter, or salty?
5. **Listen** to them as you eat. What kinds of noises do they make as you eat them?

Now write about your experience of eating lunch, comparing and contrasting the different food items by writing about the similarities and differences in the way they look, feel, smell, taste, and sound.

Choose one of your lunchtime items. Put yourself in the place of that orange, for example. Write about how it would feel to be peeled, separated, and chewed,

or saved in a locker for days
or traded for a bag of marbles
or lost on the beach
or . . . YOU decide!

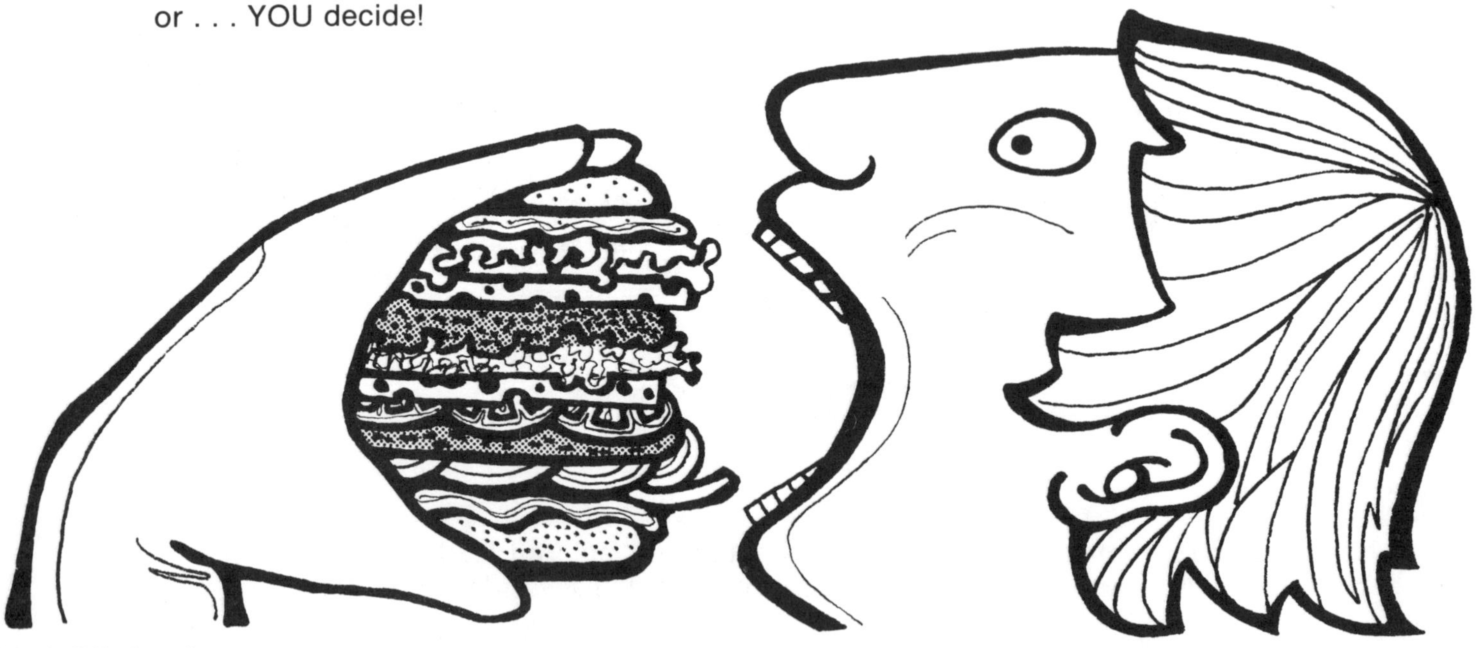

Name ______________________________

FOLD-A-LINE GROUP STORY

Instruct the class to form groups of eight to ten students each. Give each group two 8½" x 11" pieces of paper taped together.

Have one student write the beginning of a story (one or two sentences only), fold over the written part, and pass the paper to the next person. That person reads the beginning of the story, adds another sentence or two, folds the paper over, and passes it on. Each person reads only the lines written by the person immediately before. The very last person adds the conclusion to the story.

Suggested Rules:

1. All material should be in good taste and positively stated.
2. Keep the story going by including characters, action, and conversation.

After the groups have completed the stories, have each group read aloud the story with the original beginning. For an interesting variation of this activity, use the same beginning for the entire class and compare the different results at the end.

Sample Beginnings:

- It was a dark and stormy night when . . .
- I vividly recall the dream I had last night.
- I was all alone, when there was a sudden knock on the door.
- The votes were in. Mrs. Jones stood up to read the results.
- When John picked up the phone, he was surprised to hear . . .
- "Please deliver this box to Mr. Green," said Tom.
- The note read, "The $1,000 is all yours."

Name ______________________________

LEGENDS IN THEIR OWN TIME

Choose any noun. Begin with "For the want of a ______." Try to follow the noun through a progression of ideas. Conclude your legend with "And all for the want of a ______."

Examples:

For the Want of a Rope

For the want of a rope
  the swing was lost.
For the want of a swing
  the boy was lost.
For the want of a boy
  the mind was lost.
For the want of a mind
  the idea was lost.
For the want of an idea
  the invention was lost.
For the want of an invention
  the cause was lost.
And all for the want of a rope.

By V. Paul, age 9

For the Want of Numbers

For the want of numbers
  the clock was lost.
For the want of the clock
  the time was lost.
For the want of the time
  the day was lost.
For the want of the day
  the night was lost.
For the want of the night
  the light was lost.
For the want of the light
  the people were lost.
For the want of people
  the world was lost.
And all for the want of numbers.

By M. O'Connor, age 10

For the Want of a Dream

For the want of a dream
  the curiosity was lost.
For the want of curiosity
  the ambition was lost.
For the want of ambition
  the spirit was lost.
For the want of spirit
  the child was lost.
And all for the want of a dream.

By C. Stiles, age 12

Name ____________________

WHAT DO YOU THINK?

Write a letter, story, or essay to the editor of your daily newspaper. Choose a topic that you have some feelings and ideas about. Use one of the topics suggested below or think up your own. Take a stand on the issue, expressing either support or disapproval. Use facts to document your stand. If you are writing against the issue, make positive suggestions for change.

- returnable bottle and can legislation
- year-round school
- pollution
- hitchhiking
- minimum voting age
- minimum driving age
- commercials on TV
- energy crisis
- inflation
- drug abuse
- video games
- grading system
- school uniforms or dress code
- competition in sports
- competition for grades
- punk rock music
- endangered animals
- smoking
- homework
- gun legislation

Name ______________________

SURVEY STRATEGIES

Survey research produces statistics that tell how many people have similar opinions or preferences.

Conduct your own survey. Ask at least twelve people the same question or set of questions. Total your findings, then write about the results of your survey.

Suggested Survey Topics:

A person's favorite

- video game
- hobby
- sport
- way to earn money
- way to spend money
- teacher or class
- movie, book, or TV show
- vacation spot
- restaurant
- beverage
- dessert
- color
- animal
- rock star
- item to collect

The most needed

- invention
- change at school
- change in the world
- improvement at home
- scientific discovery
- vaccine, serum, or medicine
- new rule or law
- new building

Suggested Survey Form:

Pet Survey Names :	Dog	Rabbit	Cat	Parakeet	Turtle	Hamster or Gerbil	Parrot	Monkey	Fish	Guinea Pig	Other
Brad Smith	X				X						
Nancy Garcia		X									
Sue Jones			X								
Scott Chang	X										
TOTAL RESULTS											

Name ____________________

CONVERSATIONS *Past and Present*

Write an imaginary conversation between two famous people or animals. You can choose historical figures or people who are in the news today. Think of things you'd like to know about each conversational partner and develop questions that they can ask each other.

Examples:

A Conversation between Ian Fleming (F) and Charles Dickens (D)

D: I heard about your success in *Moonraker.* How did it go?

F: Out of this world! I made a few changes from the book.

D: That's fine. Others have changed my book, *A Christmas Carol.* Sometimes I hardly recognize it.

F: I've enjoyed movies made from the books you've written. My favorite character is Tiny Tim; he seems so real.

D: Thanks. I like the way 007 gets out of his difficulties. And those daring adventures . . . Wow!

A Conversation between Black Beauty (BB) and Black Stallion (BS)

BB: Please tell me about one of your adventures.

BS: I was on a big boat. One night there was a fire, and I became so frightened that I jumped off the boat. My master, Alec, fell off, and I saved his life. We swam to an island. Tell me, did you have a kind master too?

BB: Well, I had more than one master. Some were nice and some were not. Once I was violently whipped while running up a hill. My life was not easy.

Name ____________________

You have trophies to present to

- the best teacher
- your best friend
- yourself . . . for a significant accomplishment

Write a speech to give as you present each trophy to the winning person.

1. Choose the teacher who has done the best job of teaching his or her subject. Describe an incident when that teacher was especially interesting, clever, funny, or fair.

2. Choose the friend who has done the best job of being kind, friendly, or fun. Describe some reasons for the award. What has your friend done to become special to you?

3. Today is the day that you win a trophy of your own! What have you done to earn it? Consider all the possibilities (see suggestions below), and choose the one that is right for you. In the presentation speech, describe the training or experience you acquired that enabled you to attain your goal.

Suggestions:

- smartest student in the fifth grade
- best personality
- best all-around athlete
- best speller
- most skilled gymnast
- most creative party giver
- most clever movie producer
- fastest apple eater
- most avid reader
- best storyteller
- Olympic Gold Medalist
- motocross champ
- the greatest sister or brother
- best piano player
- most graceful ice skater
- best poet
- best all-around student
- most considerate friend
- skiing champ
- best singer

Name ________________________

Speaking Out on Siblings

Write about your brothers or sisters, or about how it feels not to have any siblings. Include details such as ages, likes, dislikes, things you do together, problems, and disagreements. What do you like best and what do you like least about your sibling(s)? Leave room on your paper to draw a picture of your family.

Examples:

"I am sad that I do not have a brother, but on second thought, he would break some of my toys or rip my books. He also might cry at night so that I couldn't sleep. But if he were nice, I might like him."

"I have a sister in seventh grade named Nancy. She is a fun person to be with sometimes, but other times she bugs me or picks on me. She often helps me with drawing, because I am not a very good artist. If I didn't have a sister, I am not sure how I would like or dislike it, but I think I might be sad or lonely without her."

Name ______________________________

USE the NEWS

Use the news to write a story or poem. Look through the newspaper for topic ideas, checking headlines and subtitles. The front page will have world issues and important local news. Turn to the sports, business, and family sections for more ideas.

Think about your story's or poem's

- **location**—city, state, and/or country
- **setting**—indoors, outdoors, buildings, scenery
- **weather conditions**—sun, rain, snow, fog
- **characters**—their sex, age, physical features, occupations
- **activities**—what the characters do and why

Make notes for yourself on the above details, then write your story.

Here are some headlines to spark ideas:

Name ____________________

News Stories

Rudyard Kipling, working as a newspaper reporter, wrote

I keep six honest serving men
(They taught me all I knew);
Their names are What and Why and When
And How and Where and Who.

From *The Just-So Stories* (1902)
"The Elephant's Child"

Write a news story about you and something you would like to see happen. Include who, what, when, where, why, and how. Write a catchy headline, a byline (your name), and a dateline (where, when) for your story.

Examples:

DAILY NEWS-PRESS

MONDAY MORNING 198__ 12 PAGES PAGE A-1

Eleven-Year-Old Wonder!

by Keith Gilbert

On December 6, 1982, Keith Gilbert will be starting quarterback for the San Diego Chargers. He was drafted from the Beverly Vista Flag Football Team. Keith is replacing Dan Fouts, the All-Pro, because of a broken rib Fouts suffered against Denver last week.

We'll Show Them!

by Susan Feiner

On April 12, 1983, the students at Castle Heights School will be able to teach. That day, the students will be the teachers, and the teachers will be the students. The students will teach all subjects, from music to math. They will show how they feel about homework and tests. This started when Susan Feiner, a sixth-grade student, wrote to a local newspaper about her idea. Everyone agreed it was a good thing to try, so on April 12, we'll show them!

Name ______________________

CLASSIFIED STORIES

LOST AND FOUND | FOR RENT | WANTED

Write a story using your local newspaper's classified ads to find amusing, sad, unusual, and special plot ideas. Check the Personal, Lost and Found, Employment Opportunities, and Homes for Rent or Sale sections.

Examples:

Substantial reward offered for return of "Silver" taken from home on Via Los Padres on October 3. Call 293-0978.

Found: Ring of great apparent value, with diamonds and gold. Call 435-0923 and describe.

For sale: Poem for yourself or a friend. Send $1.30 to: P.O. Box 32, Palmer, Alaska.

Travel School, oldest in the West, enrolls immigrants and alien students for training. Call 462-3211.

Free kittens to good homes. Black/white/orange. Call 634-9865.

Gift shop, Wilshire area, seeks responsible manager for night-shift. Call 838-7623.

Billy, please come home, all is forgiven. Rover can sleep in your room. Mom

Name ______________________

Mystery Titles

Write a mystery story! You will need

- the **plot**—what happens in the story
- the **characters**—with lots of conversation
- the **setting**—where and when
- the **action**—who does what to whom
- the **motive**—possibilities include anger, greed, jealousy, hate, and love
- the **solutions**—how your mystery will be solved

Consider these mystery titles:

The Policeman Kept Walking
The Invisible Man
A Mysterious Shadow
Poison at Noon
Danger Mountain
The Missing Necklace
The Case of the Broken Pencil
The Locked Box
Beyond a Reasonable Doubt
The Broken Piano
The Plot to Take Over the City
The Missing Diary
Under the Bed
The Day the Earth Was Dark
The Silent Intruder
The Missing Report Card
A Mistaken Identity
Only Nine Fingerprints

Name ______________________________

A Dream of a Story

Your dreams are a good source of many new, creative ideas. Keep some notepaper and a pencil beside your bed, and write down what you remember from your dreams in a one-week period. Be sure to take notes as soon as you wake up.

Use one of your dreams as the basis for a story, or create an imaginary dream and write a story about it.

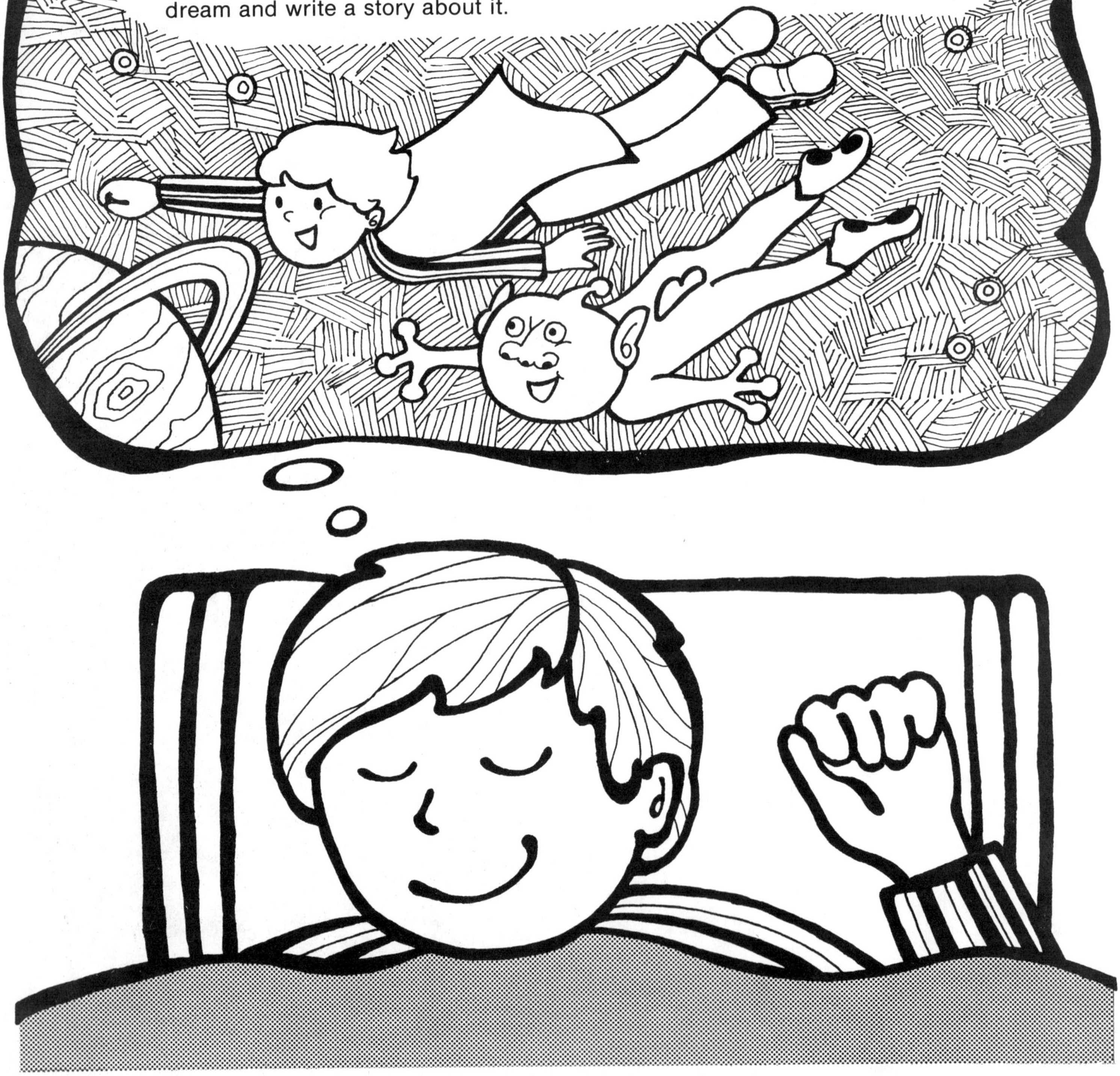

Name ____________________

FOCUS ON THE FUTURE

Imagine living one hundred years from now. What will be the same? What will be different?

Write a story that takes place in the future. Describe housing, means of travel, clothes, and food, as well as a day in the life of an average person.

Name ______________________

Pick a Perfect

Make a list of different objects, activities, and situations.

Examples:

- pet
- friend
- game
- way to travel
- school day
- vacation spot
- skateboard
- video game
- cure for a disease
- book
- reward
- sport
- way to wake up in the morning

Choose one category and think about the *perfect* example of it. Write about your perfect choice, using adjectives to describe your ideas.

Example:

"The perfect vacation spot is warm during the day, but not hot, and evenings are comfortable. There is a lake with trees and mountains all around. Sports and other activities are available, but you only participate if you really want to. You can just sit around all day and relax, or you can hike, go fishing, or take dancing lessons. The price is low enough so you can take the whole family."

Name ______________________

NOTE IT

Someone left a note for you. What does it say?

Name ______________________

VALUES on a string

Trace the patterns on page 43 onto sheets of construction paper or tagboard of different colors. Cut out the shapes and punch a hole in the top and bottom of each one except the star (top hole only).

Write your responses to the following questions on the forms, using both sides if necessary.

Use string to connect the forms, with an extra piece tied to the top of the eye so that you can hang your new creation.

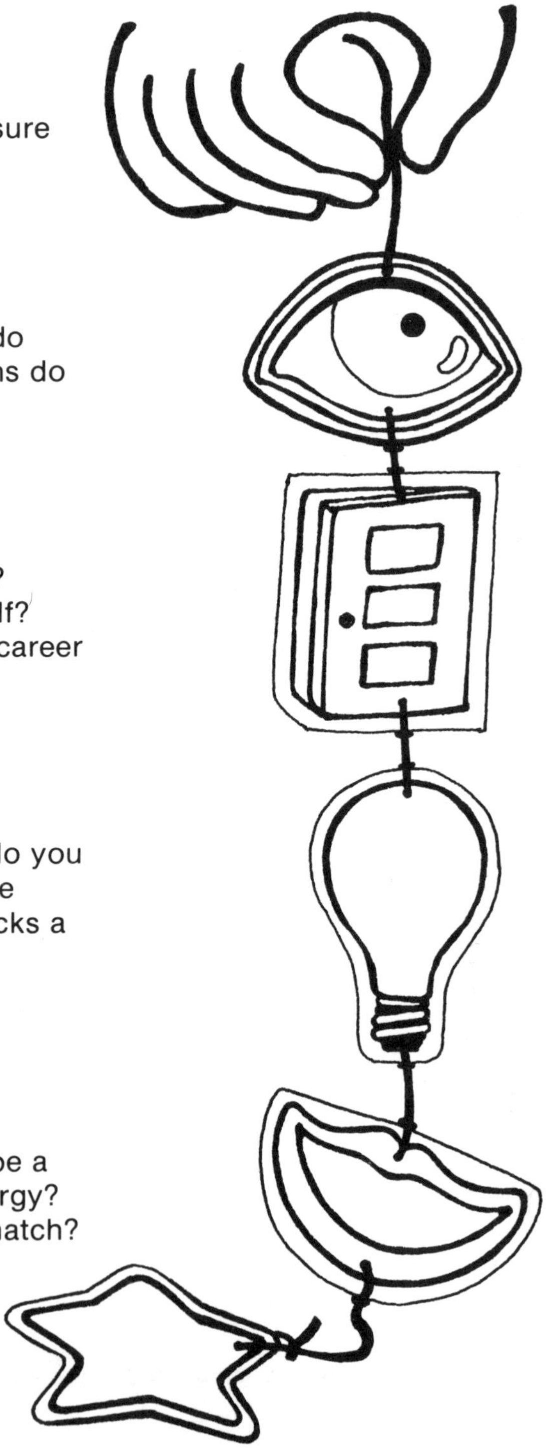

The Eye

What **truths** do you see? What things are you sure of?

The Open Door

What **freedoms** do you have? What freedoms do your think you deserve to have? What freedoms do you think are denied to others?

The Light Bulb

What **ideas** do you have for now or the future? What ideas will you be able to develop yourself? Where will you seek help? Do you hope for a career in any special field? Why?

The Smile

Do you have a sense of **humor**? What things do you find humorous? What are a few of your favorite jokes or riddles? Do you know anyone who lacks a sense of humor?

The Star

How do you think you will earn **fame and recognition** someday? Will you write a book, be a costume designer, invent a new source of energy? Will you get all A's or win a race or a tennis match?

Patterns

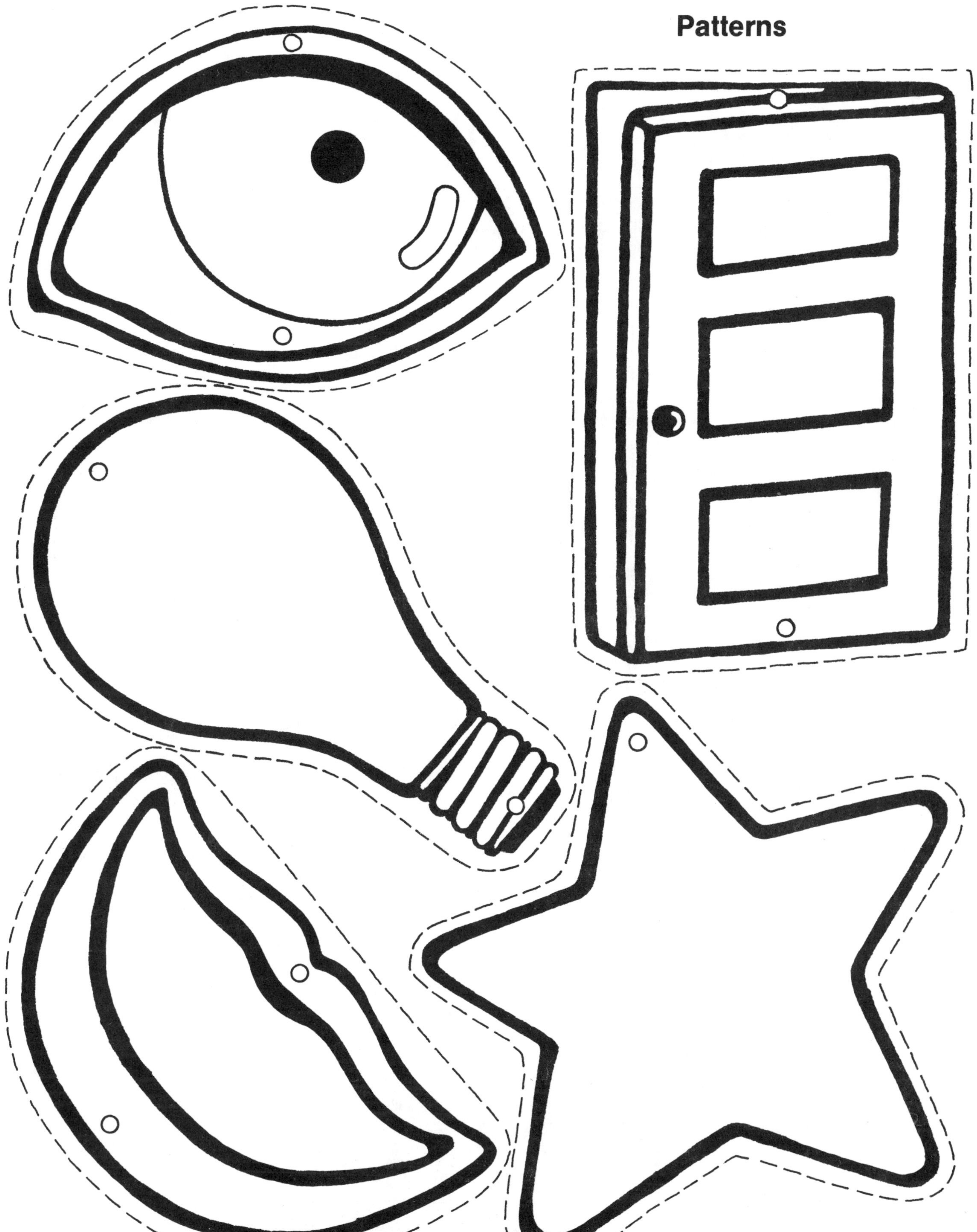

Name ______________________

Object Autobiographies

Imagine that you are one of the objects on this page. Write a story from the point of view of the object you choose (as if the **object** is the author of the story). Describe your experiences, adventures, and problems in the world of human beings.

Example:

"Life as a candle is very illuminating. I learn many things every day because people need me to cast light on what they are doing. My great-grandfather helped Abraham Lincoln learn how to read in a log cabin in Illinois."

Name ______________________________

Motion Poems

Make a selection from the list below and write a poem, illustrating the motion described by the words through the way you write the poem on your paper.

Ideas:

- raindrops
- a jet trail
- a crawling snake
- the wind
- piano keys
- tears
- a flower growing from seed
- ocean waves
- ripples in a pond
- snowfall
- an avalanche
- a spider web

Your Ideas:

1. ______________________________
2. ______________________________
3. ______________________________

Example:

Name ____________________

★ The Star ★

(A Play for You to Complete)

Characters and Props:

Narrator
Two tennis players, either boys or girls (Gary and Rodney, in this writing)
A tournament sign
A net stretching across the room or stage
Four racquets (no balls, action is pantomimed)
Towel, thermos

NARRATOR. We are all invited to a tennis tournament taking place in our town. We will witness one game. As the story opens, we see two players, meeting for the first time.

GARY. *(He is the shorter of the two. He wears shorts, a T-shirt, socks, and tennis shoes and is carrying one tennis racquet.)*
Hi, I'm Gary. *(He extends his hand toward Rodney.)*

RODNEY. *(He is the taller of the two. He wears a jazzy sweat suit or matching tennis outfit and carries three racquets, a towel, and a thermos. He wears sweat-bands on his head and wrists.)*
Hi, I'm Rod. *(They shake.)*
Say . . . *(looking at court)*, this court looks smaller than the one in my backyard. I wonder if it's regulation size. The surface may not be in top shape. There's not even a water fountain. It's a good thing I brought my thermos. What's *your* court like?

GARY. *(Closes mouth, which was open, as Rodney was speaking.)*
Uh . . . I don't have one. We live in an apartment.

RODNEY. Oh, too bad. How many years have you been playing?

GARY. Not very long, actually. This is my first tournament. How about you?

RODNEY. I've been at the game since I was five. I have a personal coach. Lately, he's helped me improve my backhand. It's pretty powerful now!

GARY. *(shrugging)* Well, let's get started.
(As the players take sides to rally, their action is pantomimed. They hit the imaginary ball back and forth several times until Gary smashes one and . . .)

RODNEY. Lucky shot!!! HA! HA! HA!
(Rodney takes out a coin, and they flip to see who will serve and who will receive. Gary serves. The narrator acts as scorekeeper.)

Write out the dialogue and action for the game. Scoring is as follows: Love, 15, 30, 40, Game.

Who will win? What will the players say to each other? Will one player be a better sport than the other? It's up to you!

Name ______________________

Crazy Animals

Write a description of the craziest animal you can imagine. Include as many details as possible including size, shape, color, and more.

Here are some words you might want to use or consider in your description.

enormous	spotted
fuzzy	solid
gigantic	hairy
stripes	sleek
webbed	feathers
claws	antlers

When your description is complete, give your paper to a friend. Have your friend draw a picture of your animal using your description.

My furry creature has five spots on its round body. On its catlike face are eight whiskers, two eyes, a triangular nose, and a happy smile. My creature has four webbed feet, two wings, and two antlers. Its long, sleek tail has stripes of many colors.

Name ______________________

NEWSCAST

Write a television show modeled after the evening news programs. This is a complex assignment, so be prepared to

- ask probing questions
- dig for facts
- organize details
- write dialogue
- plan a schedule
- meet deadlines
- practice speaking

Before creating your own news show, you need to become familiar with various news programs already on television. Be an observer. Chart the pattern of the news. What comes first, second, last? Note props, films, signs, music, logos. Be aware of lead-in statements—transition phrases newscasters use to move from one story to another. Note the number of seconds or minutes devoted to each story. How detailed is the coverage?

Decide what types of news are appropriate for your show. Will you cover school news only, national news only, or a combination of all events of concern to you? Make a list of the news events worthy of your show.

Staff—possible positions to fill for your show

Anchorpersons—begin and end the show, give the lead-in story

Reporters and their topics:

Business—a school or community business
Justice—crime at school or in the community
Education—new trends in classrooms
Social—parties, events
Science—innovative ideas, new discoveries
National—government policy, activities
World—issues of concern
Weather—up-to-date information
Music—concerts, groups
Sports—games in school or away from school
Gossip—local items

Name ______________________

FOR REPORTERS

Sources of Information for Reporters

1. Newspapers
2. Personal interviews
   Plan questions *before* you interview.
   Tape your conversation or take notes.
   Write the story. Do not plan to ad-lib.
   Rewrite or edit the story. Time yourself so you know how long it takes to read the story aloud, slowly and clearly!
3. Library—Magazines and books can help provide information to include in your newscast.
4. Television—You can get lots of ideas by watching the professionals at work!

Putting It All Together

When the reporters and anchorpersons have finished their writing, you should rehearse the show. Listen to how it sounds, and decide what needs to be cut (eliminated) and what needs more elaboration (detail).

Your newscast team may want to invent stage names. What about a logo for the station (such as the NBC peacock)?

Imaginations Play a Part

Although real newscast teams strive to make the news as current as possible, you may not have enough information to do so. You can adapt your news to one of the following formats:

- Medieval News Report
- Behind the Scenes at Your School
- Government, 1865-66
- That Was the Week That Was (any week, any year, any place)

— or think of your own adaptation.

Name ____________________

ASTOUNDING ASTROLOGY

Some people believe that your destiny is determined by the position of the planets and stars in the sky at the time of your birth. Astrologers claim that they can predict a person's future by knowing when and where he or she was born. Astrological forecasters and horoscope writers offer advice for daily living as well as predictions.

Write your own horoscope column after studying some examples in newspapers or magazines. Make the horoscopes as creative and as positive as you can.

Name ______________________________

Stories with a Moral

Read the following Aesop's fables and then write your own fables using the same titles but making up new characters and settings.

On Choosing Friends

A porcupine, looking for shelter, found some snakes living in a cave. He asked if he could join them, and they said that he could do so. When he went in with them, however, his sharp, prickly quills were so uncomfortable that they very quickly asked him to go out again.

"Certainly not!" said the porcupine. "Anybody who doesn't like this place can leave it. Personally, I am comfortable."

On the Consequences of Being Greedy

A woman once had a hen that laid an egg for her every day. This made the woman think that if she gave the bird twice as much food, it would lay two eggs a day, instead of one. So she doubled its allowance of barley.

Unfortunately, the extra food made the hen grow so fat that it stopped laying altogether!

Name ____________________

ON PROMISES KEPT OR BROKEN

Two men traveling through a forest together promised to help each other whatever danger threatened them. They had not gone far when a bear rushed at them from some bushes. One man was a good climber and quickly climbed a nearby tree; but the other, seeing that he had no chance alone against the bear, fell flat on his back and pretended to be dead. The bear came up to him, sniffed at him, and thinking him dead, went off into the wood again without hurting him.

When the bear had gone, the one traveler came down from his tree and smilingly asked his companion what the bear had said to him. "For I could see," he said, "that he put his mouth to your ear."

"He told me to tell you," replied the other, "that you were a great coward and that in the future I should not trust those who make fine promises, but will not stand by their friends in danger."

Write your own story about promises kept or broken.

Name ______________________

Words of Wisdom

Write a story based on one of the following sayings. Before you start, think about the kinds of characters who might best portray the message of your story and the time and place in which they would have lived.

Name ______________________________

You have been chosen to write a documentary of your life and your environment to put into a time capsule. This capsule will be buried deep within a special place — to be discovered by the inhabitants of the earth in the year 2084. It is important that you take great care in describing the things of importance in your world.

Some Suggestions:

- your family and friends
- everything about school—teachers, students, schoolwork
- different kinds of employment and how people earn a living
- how you spend your free time
- vacations
- major world events in politics, business, sports, and fashion

TIME CAPSULE

- entertainment — movies, TV, books, music, plays, amusement parks
- a typical party, day at the beach, or restaurant
- endangered animals
- markets and stores
- cars, boats, or other vehicles
- current jokes
- science projects and/or problems
- the best things that have happened in your life
- future predictions — people in the year 2084 may find your predictions amazingly accurate or absurd!

The contents of the time capsule are up to you. Include several photographs if possible. This is a big project, so you may wish to do it with two or three other students.

Name ______________________

Alphabet Autobiography

Write a book about yourself. Start the first sentence on each page with a different letter of the alphabet.

Stack seven sheets of plain paper on top of one colored sheet (the book cover). Fold the stack in half with the colored paper on the outside. Use brads or staples to hold the papers together at the fold, or stitch along the fold with yarn.

You are the subject of this story! Make page one your title page. Starting with a big letter A on page two, write a sentence or two about you. Continue the story on page three, with the first sentence starting with a big letter B. (It's easier to go through the book *before* you start writing, putting the correct letter on each page. Then go back to the second page and begin your autobiography.)

When you have finished writing, illustrate your book.

Name ______________________________

Getting to Know You

Interview a classmate whom you do not know very well and then write a story about that person suitable for publication in a class newsletter.

Consider asking these kinds of questions:

- When and where were you born?
- How many people are in your family? If you have any brothers and sisters, how old are they? Do they attend school? Do they work? Is one special? Why?
- What are your interests or hobbies (sports, collecting, building models, sewing, gardening, camping, bicycling)?
- What movies, books, and magazines do you like? Why?
- What are your most favorite and least favorite foods?
- What did you do during vacation? Tell about the best times. Be descriptive!
- What are your favorite school subjects? Why?
- What do you like to do after school?
- What are your favorite games?
- What are your chores or responsibilities?
- What makes you feel afraid?
- What makes you feel happy?

Listen carefully to the answers to your questions and take notes so that your story will be accurate. Try **not** to ask questions that can be answered "yes" or "no." Plan your questions before you write the interview. Ask "why?" whenever possible. Choose a title from one of the most interesting answers in your interview.

Name ______________________________

THOROUGHLY THREE

Choose three selections from the following list of things that come in threes or are associated with the number three. Write three mystery paragraphs about *each* selection. Do not identify your choices, but include three characteristics or descriptive facts for each one and involve them in at least three adventures or experiences.

Read your paragraphs aloud to friends, one set at a time, and give them three guesses each time to identify the things in your story.

Suggested Things:

blind mice
little pigs
triplets
wheels on a tricycle
a shamrock
days of a holiday weekend
rings of a pretzel
men in a tub
Wise Men
legs on a tripod
primary colors
feet in a yard
leaves in poison ivy
a triple-decker sandwich
a three-piece suit
meals in a day
a three-ring circus
a three-way light bulb
colored lights on a traffic signal
digits in a telephone area code
a quarter of a dozen
strands in a braid
Winkin, Blinkin, and Nod
a three-star general
a three-legged race
musketeers

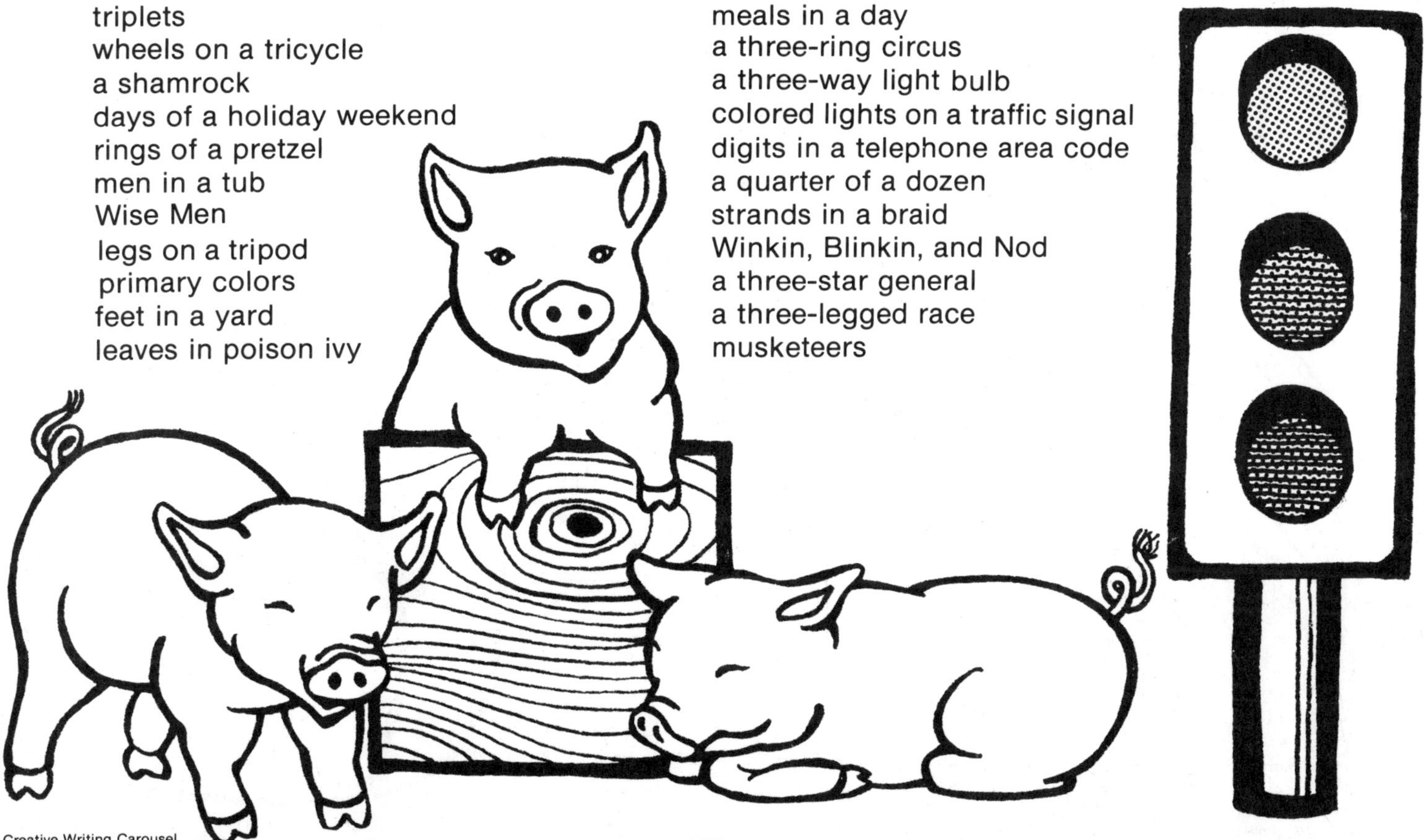

Name ______________________________

What Are They Really Thinking?

Select some faces from magazines. Look for expressions of emotion: thoughtfulness, excitement, sadness, worry, anger, or mischievousness. Try to imagine what that person or animal is really feeling. Write captions for the photos.

Write a conversation between two faces. What might one say to the other?

Name ______________________________

VIEWPOINT

Select one of the issues below, decide how you feel about it, and then defend your viewpoint in writing.

Explain why you are in favor of or opposed to the issue in question. Do some research to find facts and expert opinions to back up your position. Present your arguments logically.

Issues:

- Should students be required to learn a foreign language?
- Should a pass-or-fail grading system be adopted in your school in place of letter grades?
- Should school be taught year-round, with longer breaks between semesters instead of summer vacation?
- Should students be required to wear uniforms in gym class?

Name ______________________

Finger Fun

To work your finger puppets:

Move your puppet as it speaks. An inanimate object (such as the clock) should move only when it is part of the story (such as "when the clock struck ten.")

Write a puppet play for five parts (one for each finger). Decide on the characters and write the dialogue before you make the puppets. Here are some suggestions:

1. Create parts that require a variety of voices (deep, soft, gruff, an animal sound, laughter).
2. Give each character an equal number of lines to say and include lots of conversation.
3. If a narrator is needed, use a finger from your other hand for the narrator's part.
4. Time the play as you read it through the first time, and edit it, if necessary, to be three or four minutes in length.
5. When you perform the play, prop your elbow on a tabletop to support your puppets.

Name ______________________________

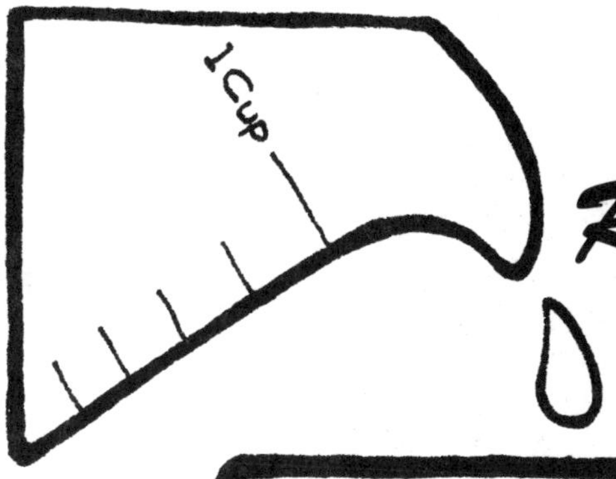

Remarkable Recipes

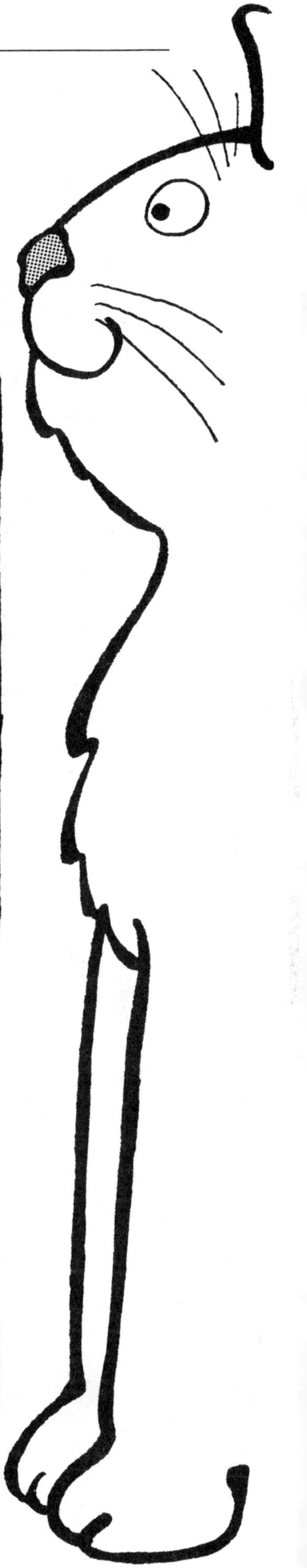

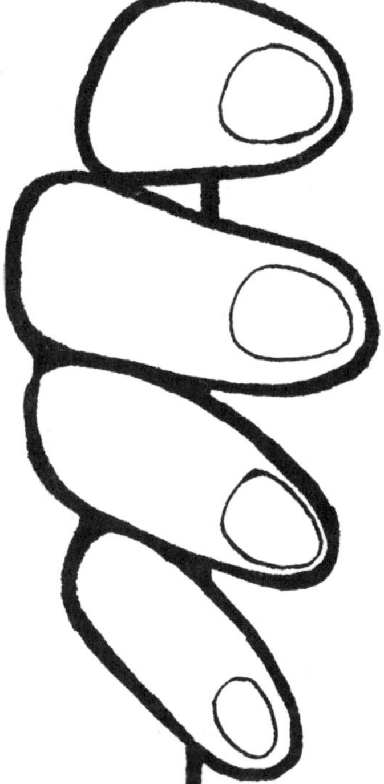

Using real ingredients, create your own unique recipe for

- good grades
- a successful party
- a super friend
- a good leader
- a mathematician
- mastering video games

Examples:

RECIPE FOR A SUCCESSFUL PARTY
(Serves 20)

3 large pepperoni pizzas
1 large cheese-only pizza
4 six-packs of soda
2 bags of carrots, cut into sticks
2 bowls of onion dip
30 tapes of favorite music
2 doz. balloons
4 buckets of popcorn
2 games (relays)
2 doz. paper plates, cups, napkins
1 HUGE garbage can (for clean-up!)

RECIPE FOR GOOD GRADES

1 lb. determination
2 good ears
3 c. spelling skill
½ T. mathematical ability
2 hrs. of study per night
3 oz. willingness to work hard
2 c. organized notebook

Mix well and combine with plenty of rest and a good attitude toward learning!

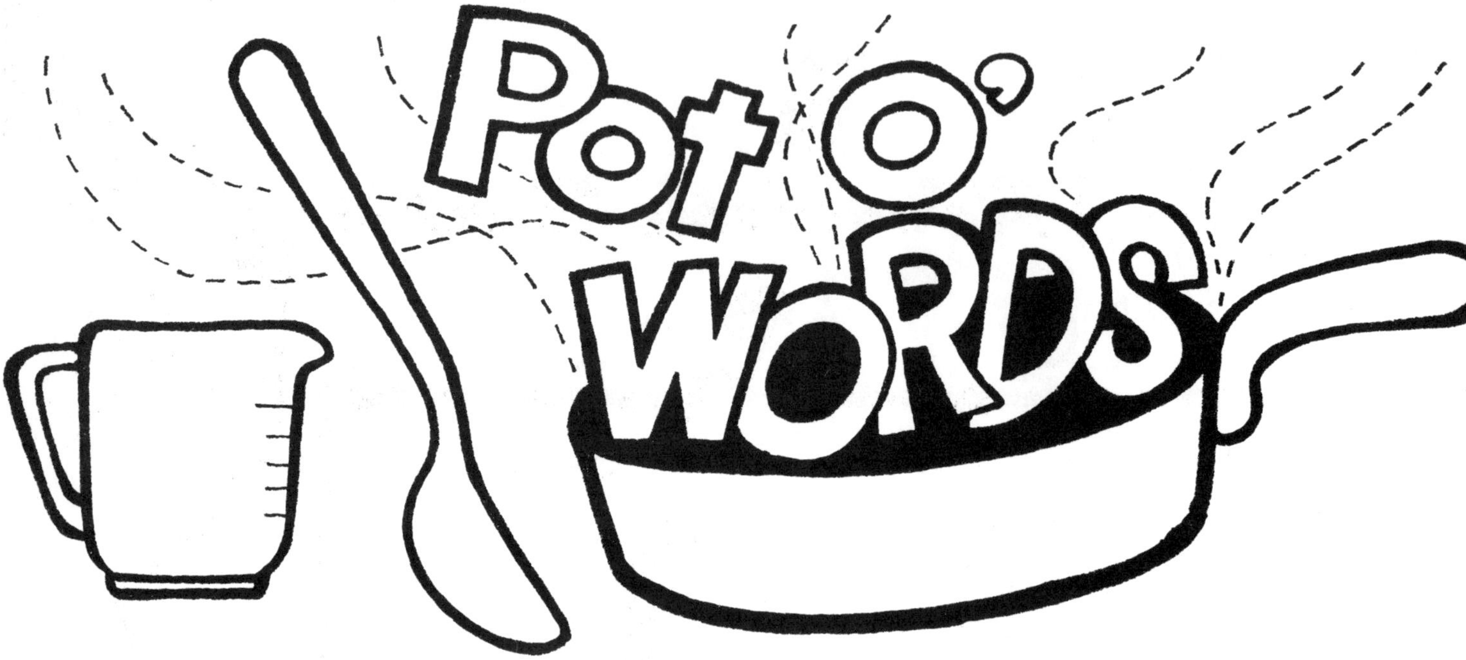

From magazines, have students cut words that are descriptive and thought-provoking. Prepare a small quantity of 3″ x 5″ recipe cards by cutting them into thirds. Have students glue one word to each card section.

When you have a collection of sixty or more words, put them all in a cooking pot and mix thoroughly. Ask students to close their eyes, pick three cards, and use the words on them in a short story or poem they can recite to their classmates.

MAKE A STORY-STARTER FILE

Develop a story-starter file containing cards with single ideas for stories. Provide the students with blank cards and give them some of the following examples of story-starters.

What happened just prior to this situation or event?

- You called the police.
- The mailman limped.
- All the policemen were walking.
- You helped your friend.
- Everyone wore the same thing to school.
- Litter was all over the school grounds.
- There was water all over the floor.
- Your parents were coming to school.
- Your teacher came in late.
- The electricity was off.
- The school bus was late.
- The siren was screeching.
- Your friend was crying.
- They paid for the broken window.
- Your shoes hurt your feet.
- You were very angry or happy or sad or puzzled.

Which—

- is deeper, an enormous hole or loneliness? Why?
- is quieter, a knife or a whisper? Why?
- lasts longer, an ice cube or a cookie? Why?
- weighs more, a scream or a bag of potatoes? Why?
- is more fun, a spoon or a ride on a roller coaster? Why?
- is more healthful, a carrot or a sunny day? Why?

Mystery Story Titles

The Case of the Broken Pencil
The Forgotten Suitcase
The Missing Teacher
The Survivors
Mr. Dado, the De-haunter of Haunted Houses

Situations

- The huge crate was in the doorway when you arrived home. It was covered with foreign stamps. Someone had pried the nails loose, so all you had to do was lift the top to see what was inside. You reached in, and . . .

- You awake one morning to find a rope and an empty bag on the floor by your bed. How did they get there? What do they mean?

- A pickpocket grabs your wallet. You run after the thief, and...

Creative Wheels

Use the story wheels on page 65 to create a variety of story ideas.

Materials

patterns on page 65
scissors
9″ x 12″ piece of tagboard
white glue
brad

What You Do

1. Reproduce the wheels on page 65.
2. Mount them on tagboard and cut them out.
3. With the point of a scissor, carefully make a small hole in the center of each wheel.
4. Place the smaller wheel on top of the larger wheel, and line up the center holes.
5. Put a brad through the holes to keep the two circles together.
6. Display the wheels at a Creative Writing Center. Turn each wheel randomly to create different combinations for story ideas.
7. Have students write a story using the various combinations.

Variations

1. Feature a Story of the Week.
2. Make a wheel for each student.

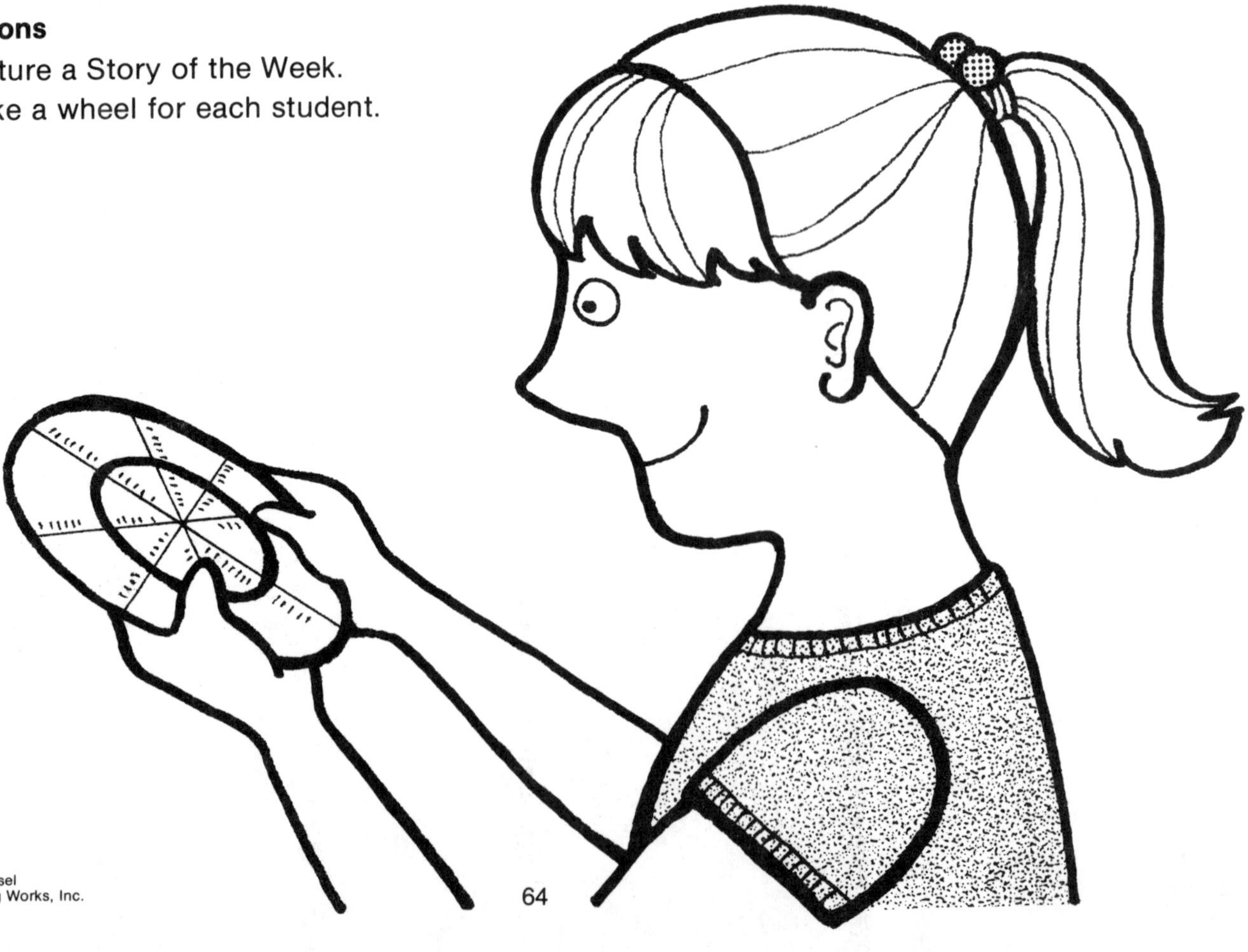

Creative Wheels Patterns

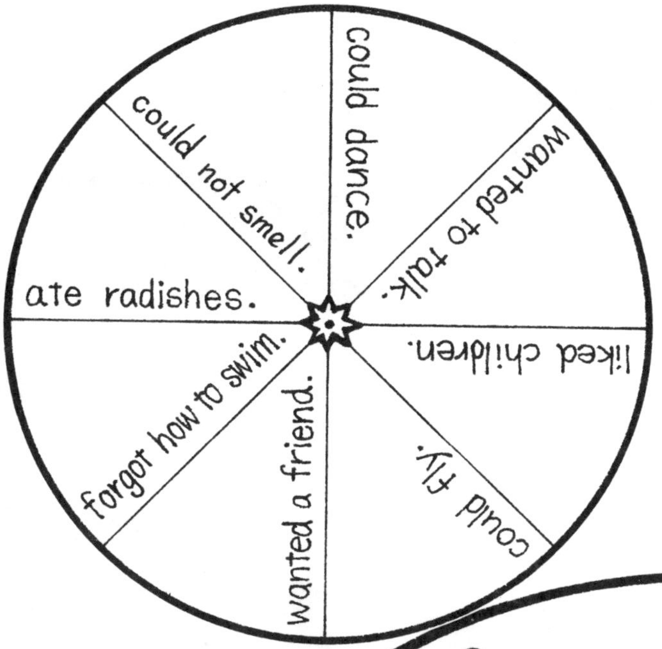

Name ____________________

PICTURE IT

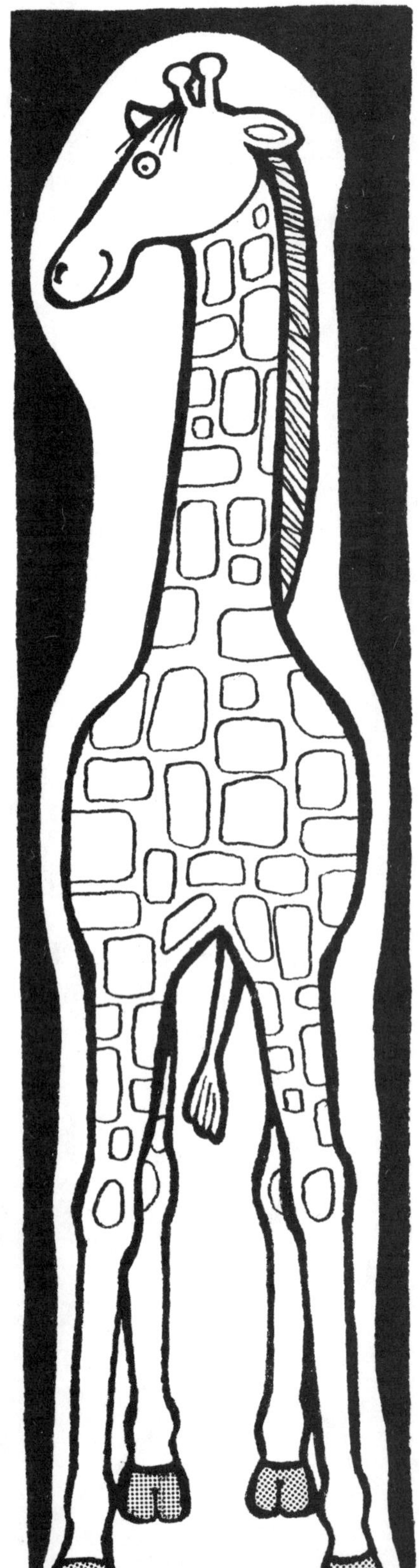

Build a picture file by having students cut pictures from magazines. Emphasize that the pictures should not have any words in them. Students should look for

- **mood**—as in a serene landscape or a haunted house
- **personal characteristics**—as in the faces of the very young and very old
- **humor**—as in a cartoon or a comical happening
- **excitement**—as in a carnival, picnic, or sports event
- **examples of skill in labor**—as in a farm scene or a factory
- **animals**—in the wild and with their young
- **action**—as in sports or at an amusement park
- **drama**—as in a fire or flood

Procedure

Mount each picture on tagboard and cover with clear vinyl to give protection from handling. Make dividers for the file box. Separate pictures into categories: animals, people, landscapes, sports.

Very young children may need some vocabulary help. Elicit comments from the children as to what each of them sees in the pictures. Discuss appropriate language, especially descriptive words, to help them express ideas clearly.These words can be lettered on the back of each piece of tagboard.

Try stories, rhymes, cinquains, haiku, limericks, and even class collaboration on a single picture.

COOK UP A GOOD STORY!

Create a story recipe file by having students prepare recipe cards with five word ingredients on each (to be used in making up a story). Each card should include a word for a

- **person**—boy, woman, old man
- **animal**—cat, elephant, anteater
- **setting**—house, meadow, river, jungle
- **household object**—umbrella, chair, spoon
- **color**—red, yellow, blue

Put the cards in a box. Have each student choose one and write a story using the five words on that card.

It's Up to You

These activities are designed to help students make choices and learn to defend them. The students should be given many chances to select and make decisions. Do not try to lead students to what you consider to be the best choice. In leaving solutions open, you help students to experiment with ideas.

Listening to Music

Have class members listen to a variety of musical selections, including rock, jazz, country, and classical. Have them listen for melodies, rhythmic patterns, lyrics, and instrumentation. Ask students to choose the recording that is the most interesting or pleasing to them and defend their choice in writing.

Looking at Art

Show reproductions of several famous paintings to the class. Have students choose the painting they would prefer to have in their own home and tell why they chose it, in writing.

Studying Geographical Locations

Have students study the characteristics of different geographical regions of their country, including climate, terrain, weather, plants, animals, and industry. Ask students to choose where they would like to live and to defend their choice in writing.

Comparing Flowering Plants

Have students study and compare the growing habits, shapes, and sizes of different kinds of flowering plants. Ask students to choose plants that they would like to be and then write about where they are growing and why they made that choice.

Thinking About School

Discuss the positive aspects of school and learning activities. Have students write about what they like best and why.

Going Shopping

Ask class members to pretend that they are in a new shopping center with many new stores. Each child has $10.00 to spend. Have the children write about how they will spend their money.

Growing Up

Have some businesspeople from the local community come in to visit and talk with the class. Ask them to discuss their jobs and why they chose them. Later, have students write about what professions they will choose and why.

Nonliving Things

Develop several categories of nonliving things, such as furniture, motorized vehicles, school supplies, or clothing. Direct students to choose to become any object in one of the categories. Have them write about why they would choose to become that object.

Watching Television

Tell students only one television program will broadcast each day from now on. There will be only seven hours per week when any television can be seen. Have them tell what programs they would select and why.

Lively Letters

Letter writing is an excellent exercise for combining creative writing with practical skill building. Students can learn proper headings, salutations, and formats while writing letters for different purposes.

Congratulatory Letters

Have students think of someone who has done something exceptional and who deserves a note of congratulations. The note may be short, but it should be enthusiastic and supportive.

Letters to the Editor

Have students write a letter to the editor of a school or local newspaper. The letter should ask a question that provokes thought within the reader, or it should state a complaint and make positive suggestions for change.

Business Letters

Choose four general categories of businesses and institutions (such as retail shops, advertisers, state government, museums, etc.). Ask students to choose a *specific* business, office, or organization within one of the categories and to write a letter to ask specific questions and/or to arrange a field trip.

Friendship Letters

Ask students to think of a friend whom they haven't had contact with recently and have them write a "newsy" letter about their current activities.

Letters to Relatives

Have students think of a relative with whom they have had little recent contact and then write a letter to that relative, talking about recent activities and suggesting ways that communication can be improved between family members.

Letters from History

When studying a period of history, have the students pretend that they are living during that historical time and writing to distant friends or relatives. They should describe their life and daily activities, including their clothing, food, and shelter.

Thank-you Letters

Students should compose a letter of thanks to recent visitors to the class, or to school staff or custodial employees who have done good work or something special.

Job Seekers' Letters

Ask students to decide on a part-time job that they would enjoy doing as a way of earning extra money while still in school. Have them write a letter to a potential employer, describing their skills and the reasons they should be hired part-time.

BRAINSTORMING

Brainstorming is an exercise in thinking. It can be used as a warm-up device prior to a creative writing experience.

Procedure

1. Gather a group of eight to ten students. (Any size group may be used, but this size is ideal.)
2. Provide a blackboard or large papers.
3. Select an object, such as a paper clip, safety pin, toothbrush, tennis ball, or other useful object.
4. Explain that you would like the children to think of as many *different* ways as possible to use the object.
5. Instruct the students not to make any judgmental remarks. There are no right or wrong, good or bad answers. Spontaneous, creative answers are encouraged, even if they seem wild or impossible. Encourage "hitchhiking" on the ideas of others.
6. Write down all the ideas as long as they keep coming. The first exercise may last only a few minutes. Do not quit too soon—make sure the students really can't think of any more uses.

As an extension of this activity, ask the students to write a humorous story about one of the new uses for the object.

Magical Glasses

Reproduce the glasses on this page and give a pair to each student. Have the students trace the pattern onto heavy construction paper and then cut out the glasses to wear during the activity.

Ask students to pretend that the magical glasses enable them to see their past and their future. What do they see? What kind of children were they when they were very young? What are they like now? How will they be different in the future?

Students should divide a piece of paper into three sections and complete the following:

- When I was very young I . . . .
- Now that I am (student's age), I can . . . .
- When I am grown, I will . . . .

Variation

Have students imagine that they can see one of the following scenes while wearing their magical glasses. Ask them to write about what they see.

- life on another planet
- inside a friend's brain
- underneath the ocean
- through the earth to the other side

A Trip in Time

This activity "transports" students to another place and time and serves as a story-starter.

Begin by telling the children the following:

> "This afternoon, I am going to ask you to really use your imagination. I want you to pretend that you are an astronaut. Your country is going to send you on a very important mission. The government needs information about what was on the earth in prehistoric times. They need the kind of information that can't be obtained from fossils, but is obtained only if a human being goes back in time.
>
> "I want you to imagine that you are going to enter a time machine. It is going to take you back billions of years. You are going back to a time before man existed and you are going alone. Once you land, I have no idea how you are going to get back, but somehow you must figure out a way to get the information you obtain back to the present time. Scientists all over the world desperately need to know what you find. When you land, think about what you see, smell, hear, taste, and touch. You will write a descriptive report. In a minute, I am going to ask you to get into your space suits and enter the time machine. When the lights go out, you are to close your eyes and begin. Do not open your eyes until I tell you to. Okay, begin."

While the lights are out, say the following:

> "Fasten your seat belts and get ready for blast off. We are beginning the countdown: 10-9-8-7-6-5-4-3-2-1-Blast off. Lift off. We have a takeoff."

Give the children about five minutes in the dark with their eyes closed, then make some sort of landing noise (try a kazoo-type whistle). Turn on the lights and quietly pass out paper or story notebooks. Give children a little time to orient themselves and then ask them to write about their imaginary space experiences.

Similar visualizations can be used to "transport" the students to other countries or historical periods.